# Toulouse Travel Guide

*Sightseeing, Hotel, Restaurant & Shopping Highlights*

Jessica Doherty

# Table of Contents

Toulouse ............................................................................................... 5
   Culture ............................................................................................. 7
   Location & Orientation ................................................................. 8
   Climate & When to Visit ............................................................ 11

Sightseeing Highlights ................................................................. 12
   Place du Capitole ....................................................................... 12
   Basilica St Sernin ....................................................................... 14
   Canal du Midi ............................................................................. 16
   Cite de l'Espace (Science Museum) ....................................... 18
   Saint Etienne Cathedral ........................................................... 19
   Airbus Factory Visit .................................................................. 20
   Musee des Augustins ................................................................. 22
   Musee Saint Raymond .............................................................. 25
   Hotel d'Assezat .......................................................................... 27
   Pont Neuf ..................................................................................... 28

Recommendations for the Budget Traveller ...................... 30
   Places to Stay ............................................................................. 30
      Hotel Saint Severin ............................................................. 30
      Royal Wilson Hotel ............................................................. 31
      Hotel du Taur ........................................................................ 31
      Hotel Albert 1er (1st) ......................................................... 32
      Hotel Excelsior ..................................................................... 32
   Places to Eat & Drink ............................................................... 33
      L'Entrepotes ......................................................................... 33
      Bapz Bakery and Tea Room ............................................. 33
      La Petit Rajasthan ............................................................... 34
      Emile Restaurant ................................................................. 34
      Soup 'Here ............................................................................. 35
   Places to Shop ............................................................................ 35
      Espace Graine de pastel ..................................................... 35
      La Maison de la Violette .................................................... 36
      Marche des Carmes ............................................................ 36
      Nicolas Tourel ...................................................................... 37
      Midica ...................................................................................... 37

# Toulouse

Toulouse is a city in the southwest of France inland between the Atlantic Ocean and the Mediterranean Sea. Toulouse is an important part of the French economy and is a major center for the aviation and space industry with the head offices of Airbus, European Aeronautic Defence and Space Company (EADS), and the Galileo Navigation Satellite System.

Toulouse (pronounced tu-luz) has a rich history in architecture and education. The city has modernized in the last 3 decades under the leadership of the Baudis – the father-son duo who held the seat of Mayor from 1983 to 2001. Today Toulouse is not only a major corporate zone, but also a favorite tourist destination.

The Pink City in daytime and the City of Lights at night, Toulouse grew up in the banks of the river Garonne. Earliest records trace to Roman settlements in that area. In fact the brick architecture that is so predominant in the city is a reflection of the Roman past. The brick buildings look pinkish in the sunlight, thus giving the city its nickname the Ville Rose – Pink City.

In fact, if one looks at a satellite picture of Toulouse in daytime, it looks like a pink patch on the banks of the Garonne. The city is also called the City of Lights because of the innumerable illuminated sights at night.

The city, fourth largest in France, after Paris, Lyon, and Marseille, in terms of population, is rich in Gothic, Roman, and Renaissance architecture. One can wander along its narrow Romanesque lanes of the old town or take a boat ride (€ 8) along the river to enjoy the beauty of the city that dates back to the second century AD.

The earliest settlements in the city were by the Celts and the Romans, almost 2 thousand years ago. It was made a royal city in the thirteenth century triggering a growth in art and education. After suffering a plague, war, and famine in the 14th century, the city's fortune turned in the 15th century through commerce.

Although it did not last long, Toulouse started modernizing during the late 19th century. With major immigration in the 20th century, trade and commerce grew, attracting major business houses to invest in Toulouse. Today, Toulouse is the capital of the Midi-Pyrenees region of France and is not only a stop for the business traveler, but an equally important destination for students as well as tourists.

# Culture

Toulouse is dotted with architecture from the medieval European period. A casual stroll by foot at the old town with an occasional café break is ideal for a lazy afternoon. Most of the city attractions are on the right bank of the Garonne. The city has 120,000 students (the 2nd largest in France after Paris) and has a strong alternative music and arts scene. There are spots spread across town that hold regular events like the Mix'Art Myrys - http://mixart-myrys.org/ -, La Dynamo - http://www.ladynamo-toulouse.com/, and the L'Usine - http://www.lusine.net/.

Every February Toulouse hosts the Festival de la Violette or the Festival of the Violets – the emblematic flower of the city. For a month the city is transformed to the City of Violets! Summer in Toulouse is a time for music festivals all over the city. The Toulouse International Art Festival (previously called the Spring in September Festival), Rio Loco Festival, Les Siestes Electroniques, and the Tangopostale offer a variety of music and dance from all corners of the earth.

One of the major events in the winter months is the Toulouse les Orgues - http://www.toulouse-les-orgues.org/ - in October. Toulouse is known for its variety of organs – 9 of the 30 organs in the city are historical monuments. This event highlights Toulouse's favorite instrument.

One can also catch a sporting event in the city. Although Toulouse has a soccer team playing in the French Ligue 1, it is the rugby team, Stade Toulosain that has made the city proud time and again. It has won the coveted Heineken Cup 4 times since 1996. The city has some world-class venues and has hosted world cup games in soccer and rugby.

The tourist pass of Toulouse known as the 'Pass tourisme' gives discounts on entry to a number of tourist attractions. They can be bought at tourist offices and come in 3 options – 24 hr (€ 18), 36 hr (€ 25) and 72 hr (€ 32)

---

# Location & Orientation

Toulouse is 580km from Paris and 321km from Marseilles. Barcelona, though, is closer to this French city at a distance of only 254km. There are regular flight and bus services connecting Toulouse to other French and European cities.

Bus service by Alsa connects Toulouse directly with other countries like Italy, Spain, Portugal, and Switzerland. Eurolines also operates through Toulouse and connects it with other major and smaller French and European cities. The bus station near the main railway station is Gare Routiere.

Toulouse's main airport, the Blagnac Airport (IATA: TLS), is 8km from the city and is a 30 minute ride in the airport shuttle bus, costing € 5. The shuttle operates at a frequency of 20 minutes and connects both the airport and the main railway station – Gare Matabiau. It is also connected with the city bus service through bus line 66. The Blagnac Airport connects Toulouse with 30 countries worldwide and there are nearly 30 airlines operating from the city.

The Gare Matibiau is the main train station of Toulouse and is located at the city centre. The train schedules can be checked at the SNCF website or at the stations itself. One can buy tickets (billets in French) from the counter or the vending machines but it must be validated before a journey. Cheap tickets can be bought online through the iDTGV website. One needs to check the destination of the car/coach before boarding as trains are often split and cars moved to another train.

For visitors it is a good idea to buy a 24-hr (€ 18), 48-hr (€ 25) or a 72-hr (€ 32) pass. The pass allows unlimited metro, bus, and airport shuttle, as well as entry to some of the tourist sites during the valid period.

Once in the city, one can use the bus, metro, tram, and cab service to move around.

TISSEO/SEMVAT operates the public bus lines in the city. Zones are color-coded denoting where a certain bus will make stops. Each ticket cost € 1.60 and needs to be validated before a journey. Unlike many European cities, buses need to be flagged down to stop, by simply raising an arm. Buses usually ply up to 10:00pm. There is a free green shuttle/bus that circles the city centre on weekdays.

The Toulouse Metro operates from 5:15am till midnight (till 1am on Fridays and Saturdays) and criss-crosses the city through Lines A, and B with the driverless trains. A metro or a bus system ticket allows free parking at some of the stations like Arenes and Jolimont.

There is a single Tram Line T1 from Toulouse to Beauzelle. It passes through Blagnac.

Night services are available on certain lines. Schedules and details can be checked at http://www.tisseo.fr/en/getting-around .

Taxis are available throughout the city with many being parked at popular tourist sites. There are many taxi services like Capitol taxis, Taxi Aeroport, Taxi Radio Toulosain. A taxi ride from the city centre to the airport costs around €20-25. A separate fee is charged for luggage.

Bicycles can be rented from the VeloToulouse bike rental stations for as low as € 1.20 for 30 minutes. Rentals range from € 5.00 – 35.00 for the whole day depending upon the type and quality of the bicycle. The Canal du Midi has a beautiful shaded bicycle path along its banks.

# Climate & When to Visit

Toulouse is a landlocked city beside the Pyrenees Mountains. Almost equidistant from the Atlantic Ocean and the Mediterranean Sea, it has a temperate climate with mildly hot summers and near freezing winters. The summer temperatures rise to around 28 degrees Celsius in July and August; the winter months of December, January, and February see the temperature fall to around 3 – 4 degrees Celsius. There is precipitation all round the year. Toulouse, on an average, receives between 45mm to 55mm of precipitation every month.

Although some of the summer days are hot and humid and there is the occasional snowfall in winter, the mild weather of Toulouse makes it accessible all the year round. The spring and autumn months are mostly sunny with winds. It is suggested to dress in layers during the spring and autumn as the mornings are cold, afternoons warm, and evenings are again cold.

July and August have been the traditional holiday months for the French. One can expect a huge rush and rise in the tourist population during these months. Holiday tip: It is best to avoid traveling on July 1st and 15th, and August 1st, 15th, 31st, because the French locals, depending on their schedule, take month long holidays in July or August, or from mid-July to mid-August.

# Sightseeing Highlights

## Place du Capitole

31000 Toulouse
Location: Centre / Capitole
Tel: 0561 223412

At the heart of the old city centre is the prime attraction of
Toulouse, the Place du Capitole. It is a complex of
buildings and a huge square which has been made a
pedestrian zone.

College de Foix - remains Franciscan friary
secret garden.
Couvent des Cordeliers   rue du College de Foix
bell tower visable

It was back in 1190 when the governing magistrates – the capitoulus – decided to build a building for public administration and a seat for the government – the Capitole de Toulouse. Eight magnificent columns paying homage to the 8 capitoulus can be seen till today. Some changes were made in 1750 and the present structure that we see, although much different from the original building, retains some of the design from 1750.

The neoclassical pink brick façade is one such feature from 1750 that still mesmerizes the visitors. The original building had a donjon – a keep (like a dungeon) – upon which a bell tower was built in 1873. The massive courtyard, one of the few structures to have survived from the medieval period has been a witness to history, the most famous being the decapitation of the Henry II Duke of Montmorency.

The year 1995 saw another major round of redesigning of the square. Along with the grand municipal buildings and the City Hall, the square now houses the Theatre du Capitole and the Farnese gallery (Rome) inspired Salle des Illustres. The Salle des Illustres is the home to some magnificent 19th century art.

The first Sunday of each month is the 'day without automobiles' at the square and that is the day to visit the Capitole. The historical Jean-Paul Laurens room, the Hall of Distinguished Henri Martin, and the Paul Gervais room are opened to the public on this day.

RUE du TAUR leads up to Basilique St Sernin
Eglise du Taur C12 - C14 murals
59 rue du Taur - renaissance entrance to former Esquile College
mediaeval house - Classical arches    No 1 Rue de l'Esquille
56 rue du Taur  vast courtyard former Grand Seminary.
Chapelle des Carmélites 13 1662

Today it is a large cobbled area with beautiful colonnades. The square is filled with shops and eateries. One can find traditional food items being sold as well fast food joints. The City Hall is a favorite for weddings and although entry is free for visitors, it is restricted when weddings are on.

There is free entry. It is open from 8:30am to 7:00 pm from Mon – Sat, and from 10:00am to 7:00pm on Sundays and holidays. It is closed on December 25th and January 1st.

# Basilica St Sernin

Place St Sernin
31000 Toulouse
Location: Centre
Tel: Basilica: 0561 217018; Archdiocese: 0561 14870; Presbytery: 0561 218045
www.basilique-st-sernin-toulouse.fr

This 12th century Romaesque masterpiece is a UNESCO World Heritage Site and is on the northern edge of the Old Quarter of Toulouse. Construction of the original church, which was an abbey church for the Abbey of St Sernin, started around the 4th century.

There are no clear records of the original construction and the dates. In 1096 the Pope Urban II dedicated an altar confirming that construction must have started before that date. 1096 is often taken as the date of consecration of the church.

Although there are no clear records of the construction, it seems that the construction was done from east to west over a period of a few hundred years, with a number of interruptions. This is because of the fact that the east walls have a predominance of stone and the western parts are more brick layered, as was with most buildings built during the Roman influence in the later centuries.

The basilica has an octagonal 5 tier tower and is in the shape of a crucifix. It is the largest church in Toulouse standing 115m in length and dominates the city skyline. An interesting feature of the church is that is has radiating chapels to display important relics. An ambulatory was built to view the treasure trove without disturbing mass. This made the basilica more of a pilgrimage church – a church that was built to host pilgrims. The church still welcomes pilgrims of St Jacques de Compostella from April 1st to October 31st every year.

This pilgrimage church has a beautiful canopy of gilded wood and marble in the interiors. The Romanesque arches lead to nine chapels. The two doorways have exquisite carvings above the entrance. The doorways are named after a nearby vault that contains the remains of 4 counts of Toulouse. Inside, the crypt has the remains of St Saturnine or St Sernin – the first bishop of Toulouse. It is also the resting place of many other saints including St Honoratus.

One of the highlights of the church is the grand Cavaille-Coll organ. This 3 manual, 32 feet organ was built in 1888 and is regarded a masterpiece of French organ building.

Admission is free.

The basilica is open from 8:30am – 6:00pm from Monday to Saturday, and till 7:00pm on Sunday. Weekday entrance is extended by an hour from Jun – Sep. The crypt and ambulatory are open from 10:00am – 12noon, and 2:00pm – 5:30pm from Monday to Saturday and 2:30pm – 5:30pm on Sunday. Hours are extended during Jun – Sep. Note: Access to St Sernin's tomb is allowed on November 29.

# Canal du Midi

Created and built by Pierre-Paul Riquet, this 360 km long network of navigable waterway linking the Atlantic Ocean to the Mediterranean Sea is a UNESCO World Heritage Site since 1996.

The idea germinated in 1500s when Francois I brought Leonardo Da Vinci to France. The plan was to link the Garonne and Aude rivers thus linking the Atlantic Ocean to the Mediterranean Sea. This would create a shortcut for the French ships as well as make it possible to avoid the hostile Spanish coastline.

The work was commissioned by Louis XIV in 1666. Chevalier de Clerville joined hands with Riquet to design the canal that was to have 328 different structures along its path. Work started with the western section till the eastern section was sanctioned in 1669. Riquet almost completed the work before his death 12 years later in 1681.

The project was completed at a cost of near 15 million livres, over 4 times the original budget. Work had started with 2000 workers, and at a point reached 12000. Women laborers were brought as there was a shortage of male workers. The canal, regarded as an engineering marvel in those times became a French symbol of power in the 17th century. The Saint Ferreol earthen dam built in 1675 on the Laudot River as a part of this project stood at a height of 115m and remained the highest dam in the world for over 150 years.

With 42000 trees from the 1830s stabilizing and decorating the banks of the Cana du Midi, it has become one the most popular waterways in Europe. The waterways, which were used to transfer mail and ferry passengers, are now used for pleasure activities like fishing, boating, and canoeing. The banks are ideal for cycling and there is a long stretch of covered bicycle path.

The Maison de la Haute-Garonne on the Autoroute A61 has free instructive exhibits on the Canal du Midi. The Musee ET Jardins du Canal du Midi, www.museecanaldumidi.fr, is a museum at Saint Ferreol dam dedicated to the dam and its creator Riquet. The 8600 sq feet museum has 6 thematic rooms highlighting the construction of the dam through models, audio-visuals and documents.

# Cite de l'Espace (Science Museum)

Avenue Jean Gonord
31200 Toulouse
Tel: +33567 22 23 24
www.cite-espace.com/

Located to the east of Toulouse this space-based theme park attracts the young and elderly alike. The park, opened in 1997 spreads over 9 acres and houses 2 planetariums (the new 280-seater planetarium is called the Stellarium), an IMAX theatre, and multiple exhibits. Within 3 years, the park attracted over a million visitors.

There is an exact replica of the Russian MIR Space Station There is a replica of the Russian Soyuz spacecraft, the most long lasting Russian spacecraft to date clocking over 50 years. There is a 53m tall model of Ariane 5 rocket, the European space launcher.

The usual park hours are from 9:30am – 5:00pm but the hours are extended to 7:00pm and 11:00pm on certain days. Ticket prices are: Adult – € 23.00; Children of 5 – 15 years – € 16.50. There are discounted tickets for disabled persons, jobseekers, and students.

There is a 10% discount with the Pass tourisme.

# Saint Etienne Cathedral

Place Saint Etienne
31000 Toulouse
Location: Centre / Capitole
http://cathedrale.toulouse.free.fr/

The Cathedral Saint-Etienne de Toulouse or the Toulouse Cathedral is the seat of the archbishop of Toulouse and is a reminder of the grandeur of Gothic art of the medieval European period. The cathedral, made up of 2 churches, was built between the 12th and the 16th century.

As there were significant changes in the style of architecture during this period, the Toulouse Cathedral reflected the different styles in its design. The entrance to the Raymondine nave is of southern Gothic style, clearly different from the other part which is of the northern Gothic style. There is also a tower which has a Romanesque foundation but with Gothic style in certain parts.

The most interesting part of this piece of architecture is that one can easily demarcate the 2 primary styles of architecture. The aisles along with the exterior and interior look oddly different and disproportionate. There is a round pillar which almost stands as a demarcating line between the 2 styles.

The newer Northern Gothic style focused on grandeur to rival other cathedrals of the period, this dwarfing the nave that was built in the southern Gothic style.

The cathedral has a beautiful Rose Window, the design having a striking similarity with the ones in the Notre-Dame in Paris. There are 15 chapels with the oldest dating back to the late 13th century. Another notable feature of the cathedral is the beautiful stained glass.

There is a grand organ suspended 17m up that was restored by the famous Cavaille-Coll in 1868 and is still used during concerts. The cathedral also has a collection of ornamental elements, paintings, and tapestries.

Close to the Francois Verdier station, the Cathedral has free entry.

## Airbus Factory Visit

Rue Franz Joseph Strauss
31700 Blagnac
Tel: +3353 4394200
http://www.manatour.fr

Toulouse is one of the major seats of the global aviation industry with the global giant Airbus having its office and an assembly line in Blagnac. Airbus has 3 tours open to the public – Visit Airbus A380 Tour, Visit Airbus Panoramic Tour, and the Visit Airbus Green Tour. Each tour is of 90 minutes.

LES JACOBINS
Couvent des Jacobins
built between 1215 ~ 1369
unusual grandiose archicture makes it a masterpiece
of Southern Freid. architure Gothic 80m long 20m wide
Famous Palm Tree roof
vast refectory

The most popular is the Airbus A380 Tour that takes a visitor through an audio-visual tour of the making of the aircraft. It also includes a view of the assembly line at the J L Lagerdere plant where an A380 aircraft is being assembled. For the aviation enthusiast it is a chance to see the assembly of the world's largest passenger aircraft.

The Panoramic Tour is a 25 km bus ride through the 700 hectares of Airbus sites in Toulouse, with a view of the SAS Headquarters and the pilot training centre.

The Green Tour is a bus ride educating and informing the visitors about the eco-efficient solutions of Airbus to reduce pollution and save energy and resources in the aeronautical industry.

Although the tour is aimed at both adults and children, it should be noted that the tour is in Blagnac and the whole trip, including the journey, the waiting, and the tour can take more than half a day. Tourists on a short visit to Toulouse should only go for this tour if one has special interest in aircrafts and aviation.

Prior reservation is required to attend the tour. For non-EU citizens, the booking must be done at least 2 days in advance. A photo ID is a must to gain entry; non-EU citizens should carry the passport. Group booking of 10 or more people require a deposit which is adjusted with the ticket price.

The Tours are open 6 days a week, except Sundays and bank holidays. A reserved slot is given to every visitor when the booking is done. It is preferable to reach before time so as to not miss the tour bus.

The tickets prices are: Adult – € 15 for A380 Tour and € 13 for the Panoramic and Green Tours. For a child, unemployed, or disabled person – € 13 for the A380 Tour, and € 11 for the other two tours. Free for children under the age of 6.

## Musee des Augustins

21 Rue de Metz
31000 Toulouse
Location: Centre / Capitole
Tel: 0561 222182
http://www.augustins.org/

Surrounding a beautiful courtyard garden, the Musee des Augustins de Toulouse or the Augustin Museum is one of the oldest in France. It was opened to the public in 1795, shortly after the opening of the Louvre Museum in Paris. The museum has a rich collection of fine arts and architecture dating back to the Middle Ages.

The brick building housing the museum was originally a convent in the early 14th century. The hermits of St Augustin were allowed by Pope Clement V to build the convent as they were living there for almost a century. The construction of the St Augustins church that started in 1309 was completed in the beginning of the 16th century.

Private Mansions. Carrefour des Changes — marks the intersection of the pedestrian rue St Rome & rue des Changes which retraces the routes of the City's principal north-south artery in Antiquity; with rue Peyr & rue Temponnières. Centre of Mediaeval City

Vaults were added to the building in the later centuries. The spire and upper floors of the church were destroyed by lightning in 1550 and were never rebuilt. By the late 17th century there was a decline in the number of monks in the convent, the number dropped to around 30 in 1680.

This did not stop expansions and restorations of parts of the church and convent. The 17th century saw the addition of a large dormitory, a calefactoria, and a meditation room.

Although the convent was declared an 'Asset of the Nation' in 1789, part of the refractory was turned to stables after it was sold to Citizen Verdier. Art lovers started putting pressure on the preservation of the arts as those were exposed to wartime pillaging. The borough council soon made way to the opening of the Provincial Museum of the South of the Republic in the premises, paving the way for the Augustins Museum in later years. Several restorations were made to accommodate the works of art as well as the School Of Arts, that moved into the east and west wing in 1804.

It is interesting to note that although the museum was opened to protect the arts from getting destroyed, the building, a wonderful Gothic piece of architecture in itself, lost some of its sheen in the process.

Private Mansions. C15 26 rue de la Bourse
11 rue Malcousinat (now Ostal d'Occitània (concerts)
corner of streets rue des Changes  Brucelles mansion

Musée du Vieux Toulouse - Hôtel Dumay

The stained glass that adorned the windows, including the rose window, was destroyed to allow more light to view the exhibits. Walls were torn down to make way for galleries. The commissioning of the Temple of the Arts in the premise in 1831 resulted in the destruction of the paving and closing of the side chapels to make way for the Neo-classical style. Restyling and expansion carried on till the early 20th century.

In 1941 it was decided to restore the church and museum to restore some of its lost glory. A courtyard garden was created and galleries restored. Even stained glass was put at the Darcy staircase.

Today the museum exhibits sculptures from the Romanesque, Gothic, and Renaissance period. There are also exhibits from the 17th to the 20th century when there was a heavy influence of the bourgeoisie. The collection of paintings from the renaissance period of French and Italian history includes some unique work like The Hunt by Giovanni.

The museum has a digital library of documents dating back to the late 18th century. There is also a photo library that is available online, and requests for photos can be either mailed or faxed to the museum office.

The museum is open daily morning from 10:00 am to 6:00 pm with late closings on Wednesdays (at 9:00 pm). It closes at 5:00 pm on 24th and 31st Dec and remains closed on 1st Jan, 1st May, and 25th Dec.

Ticket prices are: Adult – € 4. It is reduced to € 2 for groups of 15 or more. There is free entry to the permanent exhibits on the 1st Sunday of every month. Guided tours and workshops are also conducted at a nominal rate.

# Musee Saint Raymond

1 Ter Place Saint-Sernin
31000 Toulouse
Location: Centre / Capitole
Tel: 0561 223144
www.saintraymond.toulouse.fr

The museum, dedicated to the life of the Celts and Romans in the Toulouse region, has over 1000 pieces of archaeological exhibits. It was declared a historic monument in 1975. The museum undertakes excavation work and offers great insights on the life and society of the Romans through the excavated objects.

The sites and monuments that are maintained by the museum include the Roman Amphitheater of Toulouse-Purpan and the Ancely Pool baths, the Funerary Basilica of Saint Pierre Des Cuisines, and the Basilica of St Sernin. Visitors are allowed entry to the amphitheater and the funerary basilica for an entrance fee of € 3.

Excavation works during as recent as 1994 to 1996 below the museum unearthed a Christian necropolis – cemetery with large tombstones. The necropolis had nearly a 100 lime kiln sepulchers or vaults and tombs. These can be viewed by visitors in the basement of the museum.

The first floor displays works from the Martens-Tolosane village, 60 km south west of Toulouse. There are sculptures dating back to the late 3rd century. The exhibit of the busts of all the Roman leaders, lined up according to their reign is very popular. This collection of busts of Roman leaders is second to only the Louvre Museum in France.

The second floor has collections from the Roman town of Tolosa which includes some Gallic jewelry, household items in wood and stone, and statues.

An agreement between the state and the City of Toulouse allows the museum to preserve excavated objects. This made it possible for the museum to keep and study many objects that were excavated at the Capitole Metro Station.

The museum has had a steady flow of visitors as it is one of the few museums where one can touch the exhibits and enjoy a number of interactive activities. There are so many items in the possession of the museum that not all can be displayed.

Special themed exhibitions are held from time to time to exhibit these reserved items. It is a good idea to use the audio guide for € 2 as there is such a wide variety of items in the museum. The museum also holds a number of events like film festivals on archeology, conferences, workshops and tours for the children and adults.

Ticket prices are: Adult – € 4; discounted tickets are available for children.

# Hotel d'Assezat

Place d'Assezat
31000 Toulouse
Location: Centre / Capitole
Tel: 0561 120689
http://www.fondation-bemberg.fr/

This 17th century town mansion was built by Nicolas Bachelier for the merchant Pierre d'Assezat, by whose name the building is known today. Pierre d'Assezat made a huge fortune from woad, the plant used in dyeing, and responsible for the resurrection of Toulouse's economic fortunes around the 17th century.

Pierre himself was not able to see the completion of this building that was heavily inspired by the Renaissance palatial architecture. The construction started in 1555 and was continuing when Pierre died 26 years later. There is a lot of brickwork as is typical to many buildings in Toulouse. The townhouse has a big courtyard influenced by Italian mannerism and classicism.

The building was taken over by the City of Toulouse and now houses a major art gallery – the Bemberg Foundation. The art gallery exhibits the private collections of the tycoon Georges Bemberg. It has 14 rooms with 14 themes that include paintings, sculptures, books, and furniture.

Entry is free; however rentals are available for guided tours of the private collections.

# Pont Neuf

12 Place du Pont Neuf
31000 Toulouse

The Pont Neuf or the 'new bridge' is the oldest surviving bridge on the Garonne River. It is also known as the Pont de Pierre and the Grand Pont. Construction of this 220m long bridge started in 1154 and was completed in 1632. However it took another 27 years to inaugurate the bridge in 1659. This arch bridge made of stone has 7 arches but not all the arches are in symmetry.

The bridge is very close to the old city attractions and is especially beautiful during sunset and nigh time when the lights come on, creating colorful reflections.

## Rue Pharon & Rue Filatiers

20 rue Pharon Church St Antoine du Salin stands next to small cloister in Classical Style

No 21 ornate Gothic entrance
No 47 comprehensively restored/preserved mansion inner courtyard

No 9 rue Filatiers carved wooden (1577) windows

No 50 Calas house.

Place de la Trinité (Metro Esquirol) & fountain.

# Recommendations for the Budget Traveller

## Places to Stay

## Hotel Saint Severin

69 Rue Bayard
31000 Toulouse
Location: Near Train Station
Tel: 0561 627139
www.hotel-saint-severin.com

Located near the Marengo SNCF, the Saint Severin Hotel has a typical Toulouse style décor. It is also close to the metro and shuttle service. The hotel has a 24 hr service and has all the basic amenities including satellite TV, Wi-Fi, and direct telephone lines.

Single rooms start from € 48 and double rooms from € 56. Breakfast can be taken in the room or the dining room and costs € 6.

# Royal Wilson Hotel

6 Rue Labéda
31000 Toulouse
Location: Centre / Capitole
Tel: 05 61 124141
www.hotelroyalwilson-toulouse.com

The Royal Wilson Hotel is located at the heart of the old city centre, about half a km from the Capitole. It is close to the Jean Jaures and Capitole Metro station. It is 5 min from the TGV Matabiau train station.

The hotel has 27 air-con rooms with Wi-Fi, satellite TV and Internet access. Pets are allowed in the hotel. The hotel also has a private parking garage for its guests.

Room rates start from € 59 for a single or double room. Breakfast starts from € 8.50.

# Hotel du Taur

2 Rue du Taur
31000 Toulouse
Location: Centre / Capitole
Tel: 0561 211754
www.hotel-du-taur.com

The hotel is located at the corner of the Capitole Square and Rue du Taur. It is close to the Capitole metro station. The hotel has a 24/7 service with a multilingual reception staff. Parking is available next door at € 9 per day.

All 39 rooms are equipped with the basic amenities. Room rates start from € 45 for single and double rooms.

---

# Hotel Albert 1er (1<sup>st</sup>)

8 Rue Rivals
31000 Toulouse
Location: Centre / Capitole
Tel: 0561 211791
http://www.hotel-albert1.com/

Hotel Albert 1er has been operating since 1954 and is only a few hundred meters from the Capitole. It has won the European Ecolabel Award since 2012 for being environment friendly.

All the 47 rooms are non – smoking and have satellite TV with international channels, mini bar and a safe. The room rates start from € 55 for single room and € 59 for double rooms. Breakfast at the hotel costs € 11.

---

# Hotel Excelsior

82 Rue Pierre Paul Riquet
31000 Toulouse
Location: Centre / Capitole
Tel: 0561 627125
www.excelsior-toulousecentre.com

Close to Jean-Juares station, the Excelsior Hotel is a no frills hotel. Basic room rate starts from € 29. For the rooms that have shower and toilet, the rate starts from € 40. Airport shuttle is available.

# Places to Eat & Drink

# L'Entrepotes

8 Rue des Blanchers
31000 Toulouse
Tel: 0561 227825
http://www.lentrepotestoulouse.fr/index.html

Owned and run by the husband and wife team of Franck and Valery Sessa, this small cozy food place is ranked highly by visitors and locals alike. It is closed on Sunday, Monday, and Saturday lunch. The menu has a variety of beef, veal, and duck, which is regarded a local specialty. Main dishes start from about € 7.

# Bapz Bakery and Tea Room

13, rue de la bourse,
31000 Toulouse, France (Saint Rome)
0561230663
http://www.bapz.fr/accueil.html

Located close to Pont Neuf, this British style café serves delicious pies, salads, and brunch specials. A 5 every evening homemade pastry is served. There is a lunch special at € 17. The friendly service along with the beautifully displayed cakes and tarts is a crowd favorite.

## La Petit Rajasthan

1 Bis Rue Jules Chalande,
31000 Toulouse
Tel: 0561 237734
http://lepetitrajasthan.com/

Quite friendly to the pocket unlike many Indian restaurants, the la Petit Rajasthan restaurant has won wonderful reviews for its friendly staff and delicious food. It has only 30 covers so it would be good to reserve a place during weekends and holidays. A € 16.90 set menu gets you a three course meal along with rice, raita, starter, and a dessert.

## Emile Restaurant

13 Place Saint-Georges
31000 Toulouse
Tel: 0561 210556
http://www.restaurant-emile.com/

Opened in the 1940s as a guesthouse, it was transformed to a restaurant in the 1960s. Housed in a Toulousaine brick house, the restaurant carries an old world charm in its décor and ambience. There is a local specialty menu available only from October to April. The restaurant also has a seafood menu (€ 40) and a menu of the day (€ 20). It also has a la carte menu. The restaurant serves a wide variety of wines.

# Soup 'Here

25 Rue Pharaon
31000 Toulouse
Location: Centre / Capitole
Tel: 0954 464313

Located near the Place du Palais this small eatery serves soup and salads with a perfect pricing for budget travelers. The a la carte menu is from € 4–17. Lunch and evening menu start from € 9

# Places to Shop

# Espace Graine de pastel

4 Place Saint Etienne
31000 Toulouse
Location: Centre / Capitole
Mobile: 0643 653100
www.grainedepastel.com

Located near the Farncois Verdier metro station, the shop specializes in products made with the extract of woad or blue pastel. Toulouse was known for the blue trade in the 16th and 17th century which made it a land of fortune. The Graine de pastel sells a number of cosmetic products ranging from soaps, lotions, body oils to organic cotton bath towels. Prices start from around € 7 for these organic products.

## La Maison de la Violette

Face au 2 Boulevard Bonrepos
31000 Toulouse
Location: Near Train Station
Tel: 0561 990130
www.lamaisondelaviolette.fr

Located near the Marengo SNCF, this is a barge on the Canal du Midi. The beautiful wooden interior is dedicated to the color and fragrance of the violet flower. It was opened in 2000 by Helen Vie and sells sweets and perfumes related to the flower.

There is Foie gras with sweet and sour violet, Madeleines cranberry scented violets, and even apple salad violets to choose from. One can also shop online from their website. It is open from Monday to Saturday from 9:30 am to 12:30 pm and from 2:00 pm to 7:00 pm.

# Marche des Carmes

Place des Carmes
31000 Toulouse
http://www.xn--march-des-carmes-fqb.com/index.html

This market selling fresh produce is open from Tuesday
to Saturday from 7:00 to 12:30. One can get local delicacies
like the cadanet bread, fresh French cheese, and locally
made wine.

# Nicolas Tourel

13 Rue Boulbonne
31000 Toulouse
Location: Centre / Capitole
Tel: 0561 524832
www.tourrel-joaillier.com

Nicolas Tourel is a twenty-year old family business of
handcrafted jewelry. Nicolas Tourel was awarded the
"Best Craftsman in France as Jeweler" in 2004. The store is
open from Tuesday to Saturday from 10:30 am – 1:00 pm
and from 2:00 pm – 6:30 pm. It is located near the Esquirol
metro station.

# Midica

13, place Esquirol,
31000 Toulouse
Tel: 0561 48282
http://www.midica.fr/

This multipurpose shopping arcade stores a wide variety
of products. One can find from household items to
pharmacy items in this multi-storied arcade.

Lightning Source UK Ltd.
Milton Keynes UK
UKOW06f0158010817
306411UK00011B/679/P

9 781505 471168